Your First
LIZARD

CONTENTS

*We would like to thank the following
for their help:*
**Country Reptiles, Portsmouth
Emsworth Aquaria, Emsworth, Hants.
Kevin Curtis**

Front cover painting by:
D A Lish

Photos by:
Colin Jeal

©1999 by Kingdom Books PO9 5TL ENGLAND

LIZARDS IN GENERAL

Your first lizard should be relatively cheap and hardy with few unusual requirements and a reputation for being easy to care for in captivity. You can try more expensive lizards later, but for now stick to one of the dozen or so species discussed here as Level One lizards. If you find you like lizards and have the patience to keep the easy ones, move on to Level Two lizards, species with more specialised requirements, size problems or expensive price tags. Level Three lizards are species that, in my opinion, should not be bought by beginners. In all likelihood they will not be successful, and the end result is that you will be put off keeping lizards.

Selection

Before choosing your first lizard, read the chapters on lizard habitats and Level One lizards to get some idea of your options and what equipment you need to keep even the easiest lizard. Satisfactory equipment can be purchased at any good pet shop, but sometimes it pays to shop around. A specialist dealer will be able to help you if you have problems later.

Above: The Leopard Gecko is easy to keep and is an ideal first lizard for a beginner.

Right: A close-up of the head of a male Green Iguana.

The choice of species depends on your likes and dislikes, your budget (even cheap lizards of good quality can be quite expensive), and local availability. For your first lizard I recommend that you see the animal before making your choice. If possible, choose a lizard that has been bred in captivity. Such captive-bred (CB) individuals are healthier than wild-caught specimens, adapt to cage conditions better, are unlikely to have heavy infestations of worms and other parasites, and often are tame.

Your first lizard should be just that: one lizard, not lizards. With few exceptions, lizards are very territorial animals. In its natural habitat each male (and often female) has its own little area of turf from which it seldom strays and into which it almost never allows another lizard of its own species. Putting two anoles into the same habitat, unless it is big, only leads to fights or, at the very least, stress that keeps both lizards from feeding and acting normally. Lizards do not need companionship unless you are planning to breed them, which is not something to consider at this stage. One cage-one lizard; make it a general rule and you won't go wrong.

If your dealer has a cage full of anoles or geckos, unless it is a very large one, it is likely that the animals will be stressed by their enforced companionship. Specimens in otherwise excellent health probably will recover if given their own cages and the proper diet.

Lizards kept under stressful conditions for too long may be starved, have bite marks, and generally look in poor health - they probably will not survive and should be left alone. Because of their higher cost, CB lizards are seldom kept in crowded conditions and are less likely to be stressed.

Make sure that any lizard you buy has been kept under the proper cage conditions in the shop. These include a clean vivarium with a basking rock and ultraviolet light. A lizard purchased from a poorly-lit, cold tank in an air-conditioned shop has a poor chance of survival.

A Black-and-Gold Tegus.

Play safe and do not purchase damaged specimens with obvious scars, bloody rubbed noses, missing toes, or bad tails. Although such lizards may heal and adapt to your home, they also might develop severe infections and die. Don't waste your money - a better specimen is sure to come along if you take the time to look around.

A male Green Iguana basks in the sun.

HABITAT

As important as, or perhaps even more important than, your choice of first lizard is the acquisition of all the equipment that goes into making the correct habitat for your pet. What we are talking about is not just a vivarium, but a habitat that gives your pet all the security it needs while providing it with a sense of 'home', and at the same time allowing you to observe it at your convenience. You can never truly duplicate a lizard's real home in a typical vivarium - even a small lizard may have a hunting range of several square metres - but modern equipment can come quite close.

The Vivarium

Many beginners start off with an all-glass tank as a home for their lizard, but nowadays this is generally considered unsuitable. There are two reasons for this. Firstly, it is very difficult to keep the required temperature in an all-glass tank, as glass loses heat more quickly than wood. Secondly, the lizard will feel very insecure if it is housed in a tank with glass all around it.

Making Your Own Vivarium

It is not difficult to construct your own vivarium, or you could ask a capable friend to help you. First get some chipboard or similar material, with a minimum thickness of 1.25cm (0.5in). Construct an open-fronted box, the larger the better, depending upon the species and size of lizard to be kept. Now drill ventilation holes in the top or fit a ready-made ventilator. Give all the wood several coats of good-quality varnish, yacht varnish being the ideal medium. This will aid cleaning and makes the wood less likely to harbour mites. The front consists of two sliding panes of glass.

Now you have the standard vivarium. However, you can buy a second-hand piece of furniture such as a small wardrobe, give it a good clean and varnish all the wood several times with yacht varnish. Remove the front and replace with sliding glass panels. This will make a very ornamental feature to add to your home.

Lights

The basic light fixture is attached to the top of the cover. Lizards (except for some geckos and other species active only at night) need access to ultraviolet (UV) light for several hours a day to utilise the calcium necessary for their growth and well-being. Plant lights are not suitable as they do not emit light of the proper wavelength, about 290 to 400 nanometres. Buy a light that is made for reptiles. The length of the light should equal the length of your cage, and the light should fit a standard reflector fitting and starter unit available at your pet shop. If you buy a double fixture, use one UV light at the back and a normal fluorescent light at the front to provide a colour balance more pleasing to the eye than just the ultraviolet. Incandescent lights are not satisfactory for keeping a lizard over a long period; they can only be used for basking lights.

Most lizards spend many of their daylight hours in the sun, and the UV light is your substitute for the sun. Leave it on at least four hours a day if the room is otherwise well-lit, eight hours if little natural sunlight reaches the cage. If you use only a UV light make sure the vivarium receives a correct photoperiod (length of daylight) from a fluorescent bulb. Glass filters UV wavelengths from sunlight, so putting the cage in a window does no good and might cause the lizard to overheat and die. For that reason the light fixture cannot be supported on a pane of glass. There is some evidence that prolonged exposure to UV light can cause eye damage in both humans and lizards, so probably it is safest not to leave the light on more than eight hours. Certainly you should never look directly into the light; you wouldn't look directly into the sun, would you?

Ultraviolet lights burn down rapidly and begin to change their wavelengths within a few months. They should be replaced every year. The reflector must be kept clean at all times.

If you have the money, buy a simple electrical timer to turn the lights on and off at regular intervals, but it isn't really necessary. You might consider investing in a dimmer switch, to try to duplicate the natural rising and setting of the sun.

Thermometers

You will need two thermometers of the plastic liquid crystal type that glues onto the outside of the cage. Put one near the base and one near the top to get a good average reading for the entire activity area of the cage. Check regularly that the vivarium is neither too hot nor too cold.

Basking Light

Unlike mammals, lizards cannot produce sufficient body heat to maintain a constant body temperature through their internal metabolism. Often they are said to be cold-blooded, but this is an over-simplification. Lizards maintain within narrow limits the body temperature they need for normal activity through a process called behavioural thermo-regulation. This means that the lizard basks in the sun until its senses tell it that its body temperature is high enough to allow it to run after prey, digest food and escape from predators. You must allow it to do the same thing in its new, artificial habitat or it will die.

The simplest basking light is a 40 to 60-watt incandescent bulb mounted in a conical reflector. The reflector can be clipped to the frame of the cage or to a separate support. To prevent burns, the lamp must be protected by wire mesh from the lizards. Since you are interested in heat, not UV light, glass can come between the light and the lizard, but remember that glass heats up and can burn delicate lizard skin.

The basking light should be directed onto a flat rock or a low pile of rocks of suitable size so that the lizard can stretch out comfortably when it basks. Desert

lizards that are active during the day usually cannot digest food unless they are able to bask at temperatures over 32°C (90°F). Try for a temperature reading of this order. (Use an electronic thermometer to measure the temperature on the rock before the lizard is put into the cage.) By using a larger or smaller light and narrower or wider reflector you can control basking temperatures easily. Special high-wattage basking lights with built-in reflectors are available.

Hide Boxes And Plants

For safety, the basking rock and light should be in one corner of the cage, with a hide box, piece of cork bark or half log in the coolest corner. The lizard must always be able to control its body temperature by moving into or out of the heat. This is called a temperature gradient and is part of thermo-regulatory behaviour. Lizards usually exhibit their brightest colours when warm (basking) and darkest colours when cool (under shelter). The cool end of the cage is as important as the basking area.

Cover must always be available, both for coolness and so that the lizard has a safe retreat. Many types of hide boxes are available at reasonable cost or can be made at home. A simple hide box can be an opaque plastic box of the correct size (most lizards like a snug fit when under cover) with a hole in one side just large enough to allow the lizard to enter. A hollow section of bark is good for many geckos, while a slab of bark will be used by many swifts and skinks. Ceramic imitation logs are available and have the advantage that they do not support mite populations. Any natural decorations or hide boxes should be cleaned with hot water and mild reptile disinfectant at regular intervals.

A female Green Iguana. Iguanas can grow up to 1.8m long, so need extra large vivariums.

Although plants may improve the appearance of a habitat, most are difficult or impossible to grow in a lizard cage, and many are poisonous. If you must have plants, use artificial ones; they look good, wear well, and the lizard will never know the difference. Many lizards get their water from licking droplets of dew and rain from leaves, and for these you should provide some type of plant, live or artificial. Most lizards climb, so they should have climbing branches of some type. Pieces of bog wood with vertical limbs are fine for most species.

The Substrate

The material covering the bottom of the cage is called the substrate, and every hobbyist has a favourite type. The simplest probably is newspaper, which is cheap but has little else to recommend it. Vermiculite can also be used.

It has been reported that some geckos (including the Leopard Gecko) need to eat a small amount of fine sand regularly to aid digestion but, as sand or gravel can cause impaction in the gut, it is probably best to avoid these. Burrowing lizards can be given slightly damp fine sand in a deeper plastic box.

Pine bark mulch is considered an excellent substrate by many keepers, as is a mixture of shredded bark and soil known as orchid bark mix. Both can hide mites, however. Plastic indoor-outdoor carpeting is used by some hobbyists and is simple to clean, but there is some evidence that few lizards really enjoy living on this type of substrate.

Heaters

The last, and perhaps most controversial, accessory for the lizard habitat is a heater. As a general rule, keep the air in the cage at about 26°C (80°F) during the day, dropping to 21°C (70°F) at night. Desert species active during the day may prefer temperatures closer to 35°C (95°F). Few lizards do well at constantly changing room temperatures. There are only a few basic heater types available and each has good and bad points. Always remember that all heaters raise the temperature of the substrate, so if you use a heater you cannot use an easily flammable substrate such as pine mulch or paper. Also, some heaters require an electrical cable to be run into the cage, where the lizard may be able to chew or scratch at it. I advise caution.

Heating mats fit under the cage and provide a low heat that is uniformly distributed. The cable does not enter the cage. These are good, general-purpose heaters to supplement basking lights. Try to choose a heat mat that only covers a third to one half of the tank.

This Leopard Gecko is climbing over a 'hot rock', an imitation rock concealing a heating element.

Next, and currently most popular, are the various types of 'hot rocks': imitation rocks moulded in plaster or similar material and containing resistors or small heating elements to bring the rock up to near-basking temperatures. They are not replacements for basking lights, as a lizard's temperature sense is controlled by the pineal gland located under a special scale, the 'third eye' on top of the head. If all the heat comes from below through the basking rock, a lizard can literally fry its internal organs and never sense that it is overheating.

One of the best forms of heating is a ceramic infra-red heat emitter. This does not emit any light so can be used 24 hours a day. Reflectors must be used to direct the heat downwards and a mesh cage should be used to prevent the lizards getting close enough to burn themselves. A thermostat should always be used with any heating equipment to keep the animal within its preferred thermal gradient. A wide range of thermostats is available, including very good electronic ones that include pulse proportional and dimmer stats, and some can even be set up for night time temperature drops.

This Bosc Monitor is using its large, forked tongue to test the air.

FOODS

Most lizards commonly kept in captivity are insectivores, feeding on a varied diet of insects, spiders and similar animals. Some, mostly the larger species, are partially or totally vegetarian when adult, in the wild taking whatever fruits and greens are in season. When they are transferred to the home vivarium, their diets become much more limited, as the typical keeper cannot provide much variety.

Mealworms And Iceberg Lettuce

Two of the foods most often fed to captive lizards should be avoided under most circumstances. These are ordinary mealworms and, especially, iceberg lettuce. They are considered to be the 'normal' diet of captive lizards, but can be killers.

In themselves, mealworms are not harmful. These larvae of the flour beetle *Tenebrio molitor* are easily raised in the home in small containers of oatmeal and make fine treats for larger lizards. They are not very nutritious because the amount of indigestible chitin in the exoskeleton (shell) far outweighs the amount of flesh inside. If mealworms are fed in quantity on a daily basis, especially as the main or only food, the shells eventually block the lizard's gut and cause death. In the case of small lizards, such as some anoles and geckos, live mealworms can actually eat their way out of the lizard's gut and even out of the body. This may sound like a horror story, but it has been observed several times and is quite true.

Giant or king mealworms (*Zoophobias*) are better as a treat because they contain more flesh in relation to shell. King mealworms need a warmer temperature (26-27°C or 80-85°F) than normal mealworms and must be pupated separately if you want more adults to continue the colony. Mealworms also have a reputation for escaping into the substrate.

Recently iceberg lettuce was called the 'crack' of the lizard world, a very appropriate description. This white lettuce is loved by lizards. It is almost addictive - and is absolutely worthless as a food because it contains almost no nutrients, just water and a bit of fibre. If you must feed lettuce, use green or red leafy lettuce. Do not feed iceberg lettuce.

Crickets

Many hobbyists consider crickets to be Nature's perfect lizard food. They are readily available at many pet shops in a wide range of sizes to fit every appetite. They store easily in sealable plastic boxes with corrugated cardboard and crumpled newspaper on the bottom, and they eat many vegetables, especially pieces of raw potato. They are easy to spray with water and dust with vitamins, and they contain little chitin in relation to the flesh.

Only provide two or three crickets at a time so there is less chance that they will escape, and don't leave them in the cage overnight. Large crickets can be carnivorous and will attack and kill small sleeping lizards. No matter how good a food they are, crickets should never be the sole food.

Local Insects

If you can borrow an insect net, collect small moths, flies and other insects as summer treats for your lizard. Never sweep the bushes for insects near busy roads or where insecticides are used, as the insects may be contaminated by chemicals. Never overlook the small spiders and daddy longlegs that you find in the net. Anoles and many other lizards enjoy spiders, often more than the insects normally offered. Now if someone could only come up with an easy way to breed spiders... !

Mice And Chicks

Many larger lizards, not only tegus and monitors but also skinks, geckos, and Knight Anoles, enjoy newborn 'pinkie' mice now and then. The calcium in the bones is good for them. Frozen baby mice are available cheaply from reptile shops. Day-old chicks with remnants of the yolk sac are very good for large lizards that have to develop large fat reserves in the body. After two or three days chicks have little yolk and thus become less desirable, but they are still good snacks. Again, frozen chicks are available.

By the way, don't feed too many raw eggs to lizards that like them (many skinks, tegus and monitors). Raw eggs contain a chemical called avidin that prevents the utilisation of certain B vitamins, especially biotin.

Fruit Salad

This term encompasses the broad variety of vegetables and fruits that are eaten by many lizards, including some normally thought of as strict insectivores. Make it from greens such as leaf spinach, kale, dandelion and watercress, shredded carrots, little

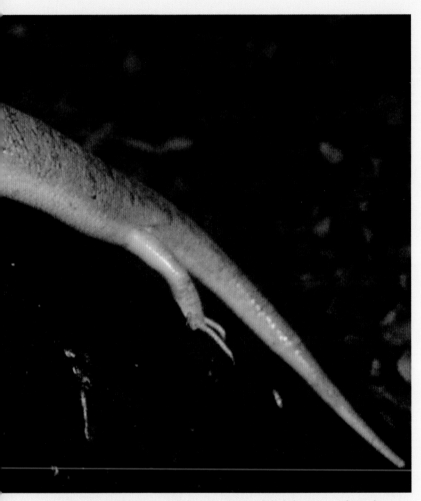

This Berber Skink is just one of over 700 varieties of skink that you can choose from.

pieces of apple and pear. Banana, grapes, berries, and perhaps even green beans and peas can be used. Fresh is best, but tinned fruit or defrosted vegetables can be used in an emergency. Make sure the diet contains the correct amounts of fruit and vegetables for the species, to prevent loose droppings. Experiment to see what your lizard likes and doesn't like. Many desert lizards develop a taste for prickly pear fruit, sold seasonally in supermarkets.

A serving of fruit salad twice a week, alternating with various meaty diets three

The Bosc Monitor (above) and the Black-and-White Tegu (below) are two of the most difficult lizards to keep. They grow very large and can be aggressive.

or four days a week, works well for many lizards. Try adding a very small amount of good quality beefy cat or dog food to the salad as a supplement, and always add the usual vitamin and mineral supplements. It won't hurt to offer some salad to every lizard occasionally, even the confirmed meat-eaters; you may be pleasantly surprised to find how much it is appreciated.

Water

All lizards need water, although many desert species can extract it from their food. Except for those species from extremely dry habitats that require very low humidities, provide a small bowl of drinking water at all times and change it at least once a day. Many lizards defecate in the water dish, so keep it clean. A number of the small arboreal (climbing) lizards will not drink from a bowl but must lick droplets of water (dew in nature) from leaves and rocks. For such species spray the vivarium daily with warm water in a plant mister, especially the climbing branches and plants. Don't spray too much or you will get a damp and murky vivarium likely to grow fungus. Watch your lizard to make sure it is drinking.

Supplements

The vitamin and mineral supplements are as important as food to your lizard. A lizard cannot do without these no matter how balanced a diet you provide or how many basking and UV lights you run. Give a supplement at least three times a week. If possible, use one designed specifically for reptiles, not for small mammals. Reptiles need a different form of vitamin D (D3) from mammals. A good pet shop should stock reptile vitamins or at least be able to direct you to someone who does. Adding a few drops of cod-liver oil to the food every week or two should prevent vitamin A deficiencies.

Lizards need plenty of calcium, often lacking in the diets fed in captivity, and therefore mineral supplements are a good idea. Provide a small bowl of ground cuttlebone as a calcium source for geckos and some other small climbing lizards. Calcium can be obtained from baby mice and chicks as well.

For vegetarians the supplements can be added to the salad in appropriate amounts (follow the instructions on the label). Live foods can be dampened and then rolled or sprinkled with supplement. One of the useful aspects of crickets is the ease with which they can be 'loaded' with vitamins. Another way of giving the reptiles vitamins is called 'gut loading'. This means that the vitamins are fed to the crickets before the crickets are fed to your lizard.

Overdoses of vitamins can be toxic, so never exceed recommended amounts. Vitamin D3 and calcium must both be present in the correct proportion at the same time or problems will ensue.

Above: The Bearded Dragon is one of the larger lizards suitable for beginners.
Below: Brilliant colour and the ability to climb glass make the Giant Day Gecko
sure to be noticed.

HEALTH

This is not the right book for a long discussion on lizard diseases and parasites. With animals such as lizards, serious ailments cannot be treated or even recognised by beginners before it is too late. Today more veterinary surgeons have a good understanding of reptile health but many lizard diseases are so poorly known as to be considered untreatable. You may be able to treat very minor problems, but probably you will not have much success with more serious conditions. This is the plain truth, and it applies to many other small animals. It is much better to avoid problems in the first place. If you choose a healthy lizard of a suitable species and give it the proper habitat, supplements and food, you should have no problem.

Condition

When choosing your lizard, look at the eyes. In most lizards the eyes are bright and active and almost perfectly round globes. If the eyes are dull, cloudy, lifeless or sunken there is a good chance the lizard is sick. If there are injuries to the limbs or tail, you may be buying a lizard likely to deteriorate in the future. Bacterial infections in small animals can be violent, reaching dangerous levels too quickly for cure, and wounds of all types are obvious points of potential infections.

Rubbed Snouts

One injury that can often be treated is rubbed snout. Active lizards frequently rub their snouts raw trying to escape. You can use a product such as Tamodine (a reptile wound cleaner) to stop serious infections, but the lizard will still try to get out. Make sure the lizard has somewhere to retreat to, such as a hide box, when it feels threatened.

If your lizard is housed in a glass vivarium, cover the bottom few centimetres of each side with dark paper to limit the animal's view of the outside world. Even better, cover three sides and half the front with the thin plastic sold as window tinting for cars. The 'dark' side of the sheet should face the lizard so that you can see in but the lizard cannot see out.

Mites

Mites and ticks often are found on lizards and can cause problems if present in large numbers. Not only do they suck blood, but they can transmit deadly parasites. A few mites are no cause for concern. Some species of tick occur naturally and can be found in special 'mite pockets' in racerunners and swifts.

One recommended treatment is to hang a thumbnail-size piece of insecticide-impregnated plastic such as Vapona in the cage for a week, removing it for two weeks, and then putting a new piece back for another week. Make sure you hang it where your lizard cannot touch it directly or place it in a small container in which holes have been pierced - a plastic container from 35mm film is suitable. Although this treatment seems to be harmless to lizards, the safety of the chemicals used has been questioned.

The frill around its neck gave the Bearded Dragon its name.

You will be able to buy only captive-bred Australian Frilled Lizards, like the one above, as Australia does not allow its native animals to be exported.

A relatively new solution to the mite problem is to spray the lizard with one of the pyrethrin-based sprays now available for reptiles. Pyrethrins are natural insecticides produced from chrysanthemum flowers, and they are among the safest of insecticides. Spray the lizard once over lightly (protect its eyes and mouth), wait a couple of minutes, and then rinse thoroughly with warm water to remove the chemical and dead mites. Do not use any chemical or product that is not designed for use with reptiles, and always follow the instructions carefully. There may be lizards with allergies to these chemicals, so you must always take great care when using them. Since mites are certain to be in the vivarium as well as on the lizard, sterilise this thoroughly as part of the treatment. Boil the decorations if possible, change the substrate, and rinse out the entire cage with reptile disinfectant.

Shedding Problems

It is possible for any lizard to shed its skin unevenly or incompletely. Unlike snakes, most lizards shed the skin in small pieces or strips, although some geckos may shed the skin intact. Like snakes, lizards need something to scrape against when shedding, such as a rock or branch. If the humidity is too low there may be problems. One solution is to fill a plastic box of the right size loosely with pieces of slightly damp vermiculite or moss. Cut a small entry hole in one side so that the lizard can enter as necessary and moisten its skin.

(Top) Monitor Horned Lizard and (bottom) Calotes Versicolour Lizard.

LEVEL ONE

This section covers the species that I can recommend to the novice lizard-keeper. They are inexpensive, relatively simple to keep, and available commercially, although the local dealers may have different species depending upon season and locality. None of them is difficult to maintain and all should thrive with proper food and the appropriate environment.

A Word About Names
Each species of lizard, of which there are over 3000, has its own scientific or Latin name, a generic name and a specific name. The generic name (for the genus) always has a capital letter, the specific name (for the species) never has. Both names are written in italics. Because scientific names are independent of local languages, they are understood around the world, while common or vernacular names differ from place to place, even within one country. Try to learn and use the scientific names and you will always be understood. Don't worry about how you pronounce them, as no two people use exactly the same Latin pronunciation.

Leopard Gecko
The Leopard Gecko (*Eublepharis macularius*) is the ambassador of the reptile world. Leopard Geckos are easy to keep, become very tame and breed well in captivity. They make excellent pets for children and adults alike and are the first contact with reptiles for many people. Unlike most gecko species they do not have the clinging toe pads used to climb walls. Leopard Geckos come from southwest Asia and northwest India. They like a desert vivarium with as much space as possible, and plenty of hiding places. They can be kept in small groups (with only one male), but do not introduce new animals to an established group as this can cause fights. They eat insects and pinkies, and grow to around 22cm (9in). Captive-bred Leopard Geckos are readily available and do not cost much more than wild-caught animals, which usually come heavily infested with internal parasites.

Anoles
The Green Anole (*Anolis carolinensis*) is an inexpensive and interesting little lizard. In America, where they can be found in the wild, Green Anoles are often used to feed lizard-eating snakes. This is quite unnecessary as most captured snakes eat rodents. Because of this Green Anoles are often overlooked as pets. They are imported into this country in very large numbers, so take your time choosing a settled and healthy-looking animal. They breed readily given the right conditions but, until it is commercially viable, the big breeders will not bother to produce captive-bred anoles.

Anoles like high humidity and can be kept with some of the smaller species of tree frog. Do not keep males together unless you have a very large vivarium, as they set up territories and fight if these are invaded by rival males. When displaying, male

A pair of Bearded Dragons. A heat plate can be seen at the top of the vivarium.

anoles show off their pink dewlaps, and bob their heads up and down. This makes sexing easier. Feeding is easy as they like crickets and an occasional treat of nectar or honey. They prefer to drink droplets of water, so spray the vivarium at least once a day.

Handling anoles can be a risky business, not from the fear of a bite, but because they are small and very fast. Always take care when handling an anole or else you may lose your pet.

Other species of interest include the Brown Anole (*Anolis sagrei*) and the larger Knight Anole (*Anolis equestris*).

Skinks

With over 700 species of skink, you have plenty to choose from. Not all of the species are available and many would be unsuitable as pets, but you will still be amazed how many will be stocked by your local reptile shop. All are very easy to maintain and breed in captivity. Unfortunately, the prices often represent the quality of the animals and the care they have received. The cheaper skinks are imported in large numbers and often are stressed and heavily infested with parasites.

When selecting your reptiles, choose long-term captive or captive-bred stock wherever possible. When choosing a set-up for your skinks remember that, although they can adapt to almost any conditions, they will soon die if you do not provide UV lighting. Some species you may come across are the Gold skink (*Mabuya multifasciata*), the Berber skink (*Eumeces schneideri algeriensis*) and, at the top end of the range, the Blue Tongue skink (*Tiliqua gigas*).

Bearded Dragons

If you would like a larger lizard to start off with, Bearded Dragons (*Amphibolurus barbatus*) are certainly a good choice, although they may be better for adult keepers than for children. They are a type of Agamid lizard growing to around 50cm (20in). All Bearded Dragons are captive-bred as Australia (their country of origin) does not allow the export of its wild animals.

LEVEL TWO

Level 2 lizards, though they could in theory be kept by beginners, have some problem or peculiarity that keeps them from being good first lizards. This category includes some of the most fascinating and beautiful lizards as well as some of the most expensive.

Day Geckos

Day Geckos of the Phelsuma family are among the most beautiful small lizards available. Most come from Madagascar or other Indian Ocean islands. The largest species, at 25cm (10in), is the Giant Day Gecko (*Phelsuma madagascariensis*). This lizard, with its bright eyes, emerald green scales and ability to climb glass walls, is sure to attract you. Giant Day Geckos eat insects and nectar or soft fruits. Calcium must be provided at all times. These lizards also require spraying so that they can drink the droplets of water. Housed in tall, planted vivariums with high humidity and a UV light, Day Geckos are interesting and colourful pets.

Tokay Gecko

The Tokay Gecko (*Gekko gecko*) is widely available, although rarely as a captive-bred specimen. Although they are easy to breed, few people bother, as Tokay Geckos are very vicious and give painful bites. Always wear thick gloves when handling large specimens. Tokay Geckos will drink from a dish and can climb flat vertical surfaces with their specially-adapted toe pads. Keep them in tall vivariums and feed them on insects and pinkies.

Iguanas

Iguana iguana must be among the best-known and most commonly-kept lizards. Captive-farmed babies are always available in large numbers, but can be quite difficult to raise if they are too small. They are imported from South America where the climate is such that they can be bred outside. Only a few people have managed

to breed them in this country. Think carefully before purchasing a Green Iguana; although many never show real aggression you cannot tell if your baby will grow up nasty or into the perfect pet! Some adult iguanas, especially males, can be very aggressive, particularly towards female owners. Green Iguanas are large lizards, often reaching 1.8m (6ft) in length. They need large vivariums and many people convert whole rooms for their stock. Iguanas can be difficult and expensive to feed in the winter, as they are vegetarian and need large amounts of fresh food. If you are prepared to put in a great deal of time and effort you will be rewarded with a large, beautiful lizard that will impress your friends and convert them into reptile lovers.

Water Dragons

The Water Dragon (*Physignathus cocincinus*) is a commonly-kept large lizard. Start with a healthy specimen and you will have little difficulty with it. Water Dragons breed well in captivity but avoid

A pair of Desert Dragons, one lying on top of the other to conserve heat.

wild-caught animals at all costs. They will always be very nervous animals, prone to damaging themselves, usually by running into the glass of the vivarium. Never buy an individual with bad wounds or a missing tail. The wounds often become infected and the animal will keep re-opening them. Other factors that make this species suitable only for those with experience are the large amounts of water needed for the lizard to submerge in and high basking temperatures.

A common House Gecko, of the type commonly seen in Mediterranean countries.

LEVEL THREE

All of the following species should be kept by experienced reptile keepers only. Don't take on anything that you cannot handle or care for, however cheap and inviting it appears at the time.

Chameleons

Many species of chameleon are available in the hobby, a few of which are now being bred in captivity in large numbers. Although such species have become easier to keep they are still quite difficult and require many hours of care. Unless you are sure you have the time and experience, avoid keeping chameleons.

Tegus

Tegus originated in the United States. They are very large lizards, growing up to 1.5m (5ft) long. Although some people do manage to tame them, most tegus remain aggressive. They have very powerful jaws and will twist around, as well as using their claws once they have hold!

Tegus need large enclosures and a basking site. In the wild they eat carrion; in captivity this is replaced by defrosted rats, mice and day-old chicks.

The species most commonly seen in reptile shops is the Golden Tegu (*Tupinambis teguixin*) and its other form, the Black-and-White Tegu.

Monitors

Monitors are very similar to tegus but come from Africa and Asia as opposed to the United States. Their care is the same as for tegus. Again, they can grow extremely large and very nasty and really should only be handled by experts.

Monkey Tailed Skinks

These beautiful, slow and graceful skinks are becoming more and more popular. Although many seem to enjoy being handled, they can inflict very serious wounds if they decide to bite. These animals require a high level of humidity, tall vivariums and a herbivorous diet with occasional treats of chopped meat. Monkey Tailed Skinks (*Corucia zebrata*) need a considerable amount of time and care and are relatively expensive. Gain plenty of experience before trying to keep these lizards.

CLUBS AND SOCIETIES

When you have been active in lizards for a while, you may want to meet other people with similar interests. A specialist dealer in your area should know if other local hobbyists meet as a club, and also if there is a regional herpetological society nearby. By making contact with other hobbyists you have a chance not only to talk lizards but also buy or trade for lizards which are difficult to get from pet shops or dealers.

Your local zoo or university biology department may be able to put you in contact with herpetological societies if no one else can help. There are many herpetological societies around the country and you are sure to find at least one to suit your needs. Most societies organise trips to the large trade shows, giving you the opportunity to buy equipment and animals. You will benefit from meeting other lizard owners and sharing experiences. One very satisfying achievement is when you can help other lizard owners with their problems.

Green Iguanas mating. You can think about breeding from your own lizards when you are more experienced.

BIBLIOGRAPHY

BREEDING AND KEEPING GECKOS
John Coborn
ISBN 0-79380-134-6
TFH LR-109
These attractive lizards have enjoyed a rise in popularity over the past decade. This book, aimed at enthusiasts with an interest in herpetology or natural history, gives a detailed account of the gecko. The final section of the book, Geckos of the World, details the natural range, habitats, and captive care of a variety of geckos world-wide.
Hardcover: 170mm x 252cm, 160 pages, illustrated throughout with colour photos.

**REPTILES AND AMPHIBIANS - CARE •
BEHAVIOR • REPRODUCTION**
Elke Zimmermann
ISBN 0-86622-541-2
TFH PS-876
This book, written with the serious hobbyist in mind, covers nearly 100 species in detail and gives basic information about many more, dealing with such areas as identification, care and breeding.
Hardcover: 168mm x 235mm, 384 pages, 175 colour photos.

REPTILE DISEASES
Rolf Hackbarth
ISBN 0-86622-824-1
TFH KW-197
A basic manual for the reptile hobbyist.
Hardcover: 140mm x 225mm, 128 pages, 121 colour photos.

IGUANAS AS A HOBBY
Shelly K Ferrel
ISBN 0-86622-384-3
TFH TT025
All the amateur needs to know about keeping iguanas successfully. Illustrated throughout with colour photographs.
Softcover: 170mm x 250mm, 96 pages, 78 colour photos.

**ENCYCLOPEDIA OF REPTILES
AND AMPHIBIANS**
John F Breen
ISBN 0-876666-220-3
TFH H-935
Covering the entire group of reptiles and amphibians, this encyclopedia provides a reference to all aspects of identification and care.
Hardcover: 140mm x 210mm, 576 pages, illustrated with over 250 colour photos and many black and white illustrations.

FEEDING INSECT-EATING LIZARDS
David J Zoffer
ISBN 0-79380-268-7
TFH RE-121
If you have decided to keep lizards, you will obviously have to feed them! This book tells you how to feed your insect-eating lizards, detailing the nutritional needs of the various species, suitable food, and how to breed the food. Treatments for nutritional disorders are also discussed.
Softcover: 170mm x 253mm, 64 pages, illustrated throughout with colour photos.